BRITAIN IN OLD PHOTOGRAPHS

SAFFRON WALDEN

LEN POLE

SUTTON PUBLISHING LIMITED

Sutton Publishing Limited
Phoenix Mill · Thrupp · Stroud
Gloucestershire · GL5 2BU

First published 1997

Cover photographs: *front*: War Savings
Committee outside Saffron Walden Corn
Exchange in March 1918; *back*: Walden Fire
Brigade, *c.* 1870.

British Library Cataloguing in Publication Data
A catalogue record for this book is available from the
British Library.

ISBN 0-7509-0853-X

Typeset in 10/12 Perpetua.
Typesetting and origination by
Sutton Publishing Limited.
Printed in Great Britain by
Ebenezer Baylis, Worcester.

The most renowned view of the town, looking south from Windmill Hill. The parish church, the houses
in Bridge End, and the top of a malting chimney behind the buildings on the left side of Bridge Street are
all visible in this view, *c.* 1910.

CONTENTS

Looking down Bridge Street. A cart loaded with barrels has stopped outside Fred Pitstow's shop.

INTRODUCTION

This volume is a selection of images of Saffron Walden, covering the town and its immediate surroundings from the 1850s to the 1990s. With its narrow streets and ancient houses, Saffron Walden is the quintessential English market town. Bypassed by the direct results of the Industrial Revolution, it has retained many elements of its medieval street pattern; there is much to delight the eye, both open to view and tucked away, and fortunately for us much of it has been preserved, both on glass and on film. All these photographs are literally stills from particular moments in the activities surrounding businesses, street scenes, events and people usually in their everyday lives. I have tried to link them where appropriate and present them chronologically in some sections, but no attempt has been made to form them into a narrative. Clearly, although there is history in every image, this book does not in any way represent a history of the town, even in the last 150 years. I have tried not to duplicate shots which have recently appeared in print elsewhere, or are about to be published; however, a certain amount of overlap is unavoidable. I have made every attempt to contact copyright holders where possible but I realise there may be some gaps for which I apologise.

These photographs are taken from the collections in the Saffron Walden Museum. The museum was started in 1832, seven years before the photographic process was invented, let alone became a popular medium for recording the passing scene. It took another fifty years or so before the museum began to record the photographs it had been haphazardly amassing, even though one or two date back to the early days of the wet plate process, first developed in 1851. Since the early years of the present century, photographers have from time to time donated some of their original images. One such was Samuel Wenman, a local bank manager who spent all his spare time in the 1920s and 1930s riding around the town and local villages on his bicycle with his camera. Examples of the work of most professional photographers are also represented in the collections, from John Mallows Youngman, who took the earliest views of the new Corn Exchange and the Market Square in the 1850s, to the successive occupants of the shops and studio at 6 Gold Street – first F.T. Day in the 1870s, then William Hobbs until 1897, followed by W. Frost Wilson until about 1910, then Horace Mansell and

E. Underwood until the end of the 1920s, and lastly W. Davies until the Second World War. The latter two published many of their prints as postcards, Underwood in particular not only his own but also those he had inherited from the previous owners of his stock in trade. Elsewhere Walter Francis practised in the High Street between about 1890 and 1906, and Galley operated from premises in London Road from the turn of the century until at least 1914. Other photographers whose work is in the collections from about the same time include Newland Talbot, Chester Vaughan and Henry Hillen. Publishers of photographs included Youngman, in the shop on the corner of the Market Place beside the Town Hall from about 1854 until 1875, Boardman between 1875 and 1888, Roberts from 1888 until 1896 and Thompson from 1896 until 1914. Elsewhere, Guy in Cross Street, and Mansell as well as Hart in King Street, were all printers of postcards. Even though there are approximately two thousand historic photographs in the museum's collection, the coverage and the information are far from complete. One photographer in particular not recorded in the museum's collection is J. Humphrey, mentioned in trade directories in the early 1870s as working in Copt Hall, Ashdon Road.

The present town started as a small village in the valley, surrounded by rich farmland first tilled by Celtic farmers before the Roman occupation. More than a thousand years ago, it began to grow into 'Weala-denu', a prosperous community of Saxon-speaking farmers, merchants and traders, from time to time part of the Danelaw and subject to Viking control. The invasion of William of Normandy eventually brought changes and new allegiances: an alien fortification in the forbidding shape of Walden Castle and a bigger church, both built on the hill dominating the Saxons in the valley. The Norman lords of the manor and the wealthy medieval landowners established a market, built a priory (later upgraded to become Walden Abbey), rebuilt the church in stone, and obtained a charter from the lord of the manor to avoid paying taxes. The village was overlain by a new town of well-built timbered houses, some of which survive today. There was wealth in the area of 'Chipping', or market, Walden, although concentrated in only a few hands. Prosperity seldom faltered, since the crops always grew, whether grass for the sheep, wheat, barley or *crocus sativus*, the little autumn flower yielding saffron which people came from all over the country to buy. Saffron became synonymous with the town because it was rare and precious. It was used as a medicine and in cooking as well as being the source of a rich yellow dye. Though successfully trading in it, sufficiently so to change the town's name, the community was never solely dependent on it. Just as well, because it was a fitful commodity; an early October frost and the crop could be wiped out overnight. As soon as more dependable sources from southern Europe became more easily available, the local trade waned. By about 1720, when George I stopped at Audley End and a traditional gift was required, the burghers of Walden had to rush to Bishop's Stortford to buy saffron; what ignominy! Audley End at that time was one of the largest houses in England. Built on the site of Walden Abbey between 1603 and 1616 by Thomas Howard, Earl of Suffolk, Treasurer to James I, the house was always too large to maintain. It was two-thirds demolished and then partly reconstructed in the eighteenth century. Its present size gives an idea of its former enormity.

In the nineteenth century the friendly influence of Quakers became dominant. The most influential family was the Gibsons. They became the major benefactors of the town. There are several buildings which testify to their public-spirited influence and generosity: the Museum, the Town Hall, the Friends School, the Training College (now Bell College), and the rebuilt nineteenth-century almshouses. The family established the Saffron Walden and North Essex Bank, later Gibson, Tuke and Gibson's, having made a fortune from malting and brewing. The growth of London and its insatiable thirst in the eighteenth century had encouraged beer-making in the provinces, especially in such lush arable land as existed in north-west Essex, where malting barley grew well. In the 1830s over thirty maltings and breweries thrived in the town. Although few survive, the building of the Corn Exchange in the Market Place in 1848 on the site of the medieval timber-framed Woolcombers Hall, symbolized the dominance of cereal crops then, just as its present use as the Library and Arts Centre now characterises the importance paid to learning and leisure activities.

Gradual, rather than cataclysmic change, visible in its real dimensions only decades later, has been a significant element in the development of the town. It has never been sacked, bombed or gutted by fire. Perhaps the preservation of the medieval core is the indirect result of the closure of the unprofitable rail link through Saffron Walden to Audley End, sparing the town the worst effects of post-war 'development'. Medieval Walden traders transported from the 1500s to the late twentieth century would be able to recognize many elements of their town. They would be familiar with some of the buildings, even if their uses may have changed, such as the present Cross Keys, Corner Cupboard, the Hoops, the Youth Hostel and most of Bridge Street, and the buildings on the four corners of the crossing where Market Hill meets Church Street. Stripped of their eighteenth- and nineteenth-century brick frontages, many of the houses on the High Street would also be recognizable. The traders would have found the Town Hall a curiosity, however; eighteenth-century brickwork overlaid with mock timbering on an exotic colonnade of stone arches. The time-travellers from those centuries would be astounded to see in what high regard education was held, to judge from the number of schools and the amount of space taken up by their playing fields; and yet how ruthlessly the town-house gardens had been built on, with rows of small houses, even some stables and outhouses fit only for the pigs now being used for people! They might be mystified that the Common has survived almost intact but for the inevitable car-park. Wonderful and curious, they would think, that the mighty parish church, the largest in Essex,

View over the town photographed by F.T. Day, probably from the roof of the parish church, 1874. The building with scaffolding is Barclays Bank, then being built as the headquarters of Gibson, Tuke and Gibson's Bank. The tall conical structure is part of the town maltings, in what is now Emson Close, which were demolished in 1950. In the nineteenth century there were over thirty maltings in the town.

should have grown a steeple, or the earth maze survived at all. Little would such visitors know that there is not one but two mazes in the town, the more recent planted in the 1850s in Bridge End Gardens, a copy of the one at Hampton Court.

There are many surprises for the sharp-eyed visitor to enjoy, and perhaps record for posterity in photographic form — tiny well-tended gardens in the tucked-away courtyards; back-house roofscapes of heaped-up tiled gables; the narrow flash of an unexpected hillside between jostling town houses; the tessellated patterning of pargetted plaster; Polynesian masterpieces in the town's amazing museum. These are some of the many images waiting to be gleaned and savoured within the pages of this book. I hope the enjoyment readers will derive from this volume will match the fun I have had in putting it together.

BUSINESSES

Saffron Walden owes its existence as a town to trade. As a market town, it has supported the usual range of trades and small manufacturing businesses. The nineteenth-century town provided a typical commercial mix that would astound its late twentieth-century inhabitants. Not merely its own gas supply and three iron foundries, but agricultural implement makers and horticultural nurseries, to name a few, of a variety to rival any in much bigger towns.

The drive and resourcefulness of the townspeople has continued throughout the centuries, from Humphrey de Bohun who developed the idea of putting a town here in the thirteenth century, to the anonymous entrepreneurs of the trade in saffron. From Dame Johanne Bradbury, pioneering education for the town, to John Harvey, wealthy rope-maker and his four gifted, well-educated sons. From the ingenious Henry Winstanley, engraver, lighthouse designer and inveterate practical joker, to George Gibson and his descendants, maltsters, bankers and benefactors, to Joseph Scruby, wine and spirit merchant, to Joseph Bell, builder, to Ernest de Vigier, inventor of Acrow props, to William Chater, horticulturalist, all the way to today's business men and women, from cabinet-makers to electronics specialists, all of whom have contributed to the development of the town.

Typical of the times, the town now offers more estate agents, antique and gift shops than provision merchants, mongers, factors and purveyors. If the town's motto '*deo adjuvante floremus*' (by God's help we flourish) is not to become a hollow jest, the community will have to fight as it has fought before to retain its individuality, or a new motto may become more appropriate – 'by apathy we wither'!

The sheep and cattle market, held in Cheffins sale yard, which survived until 1983. The yard was constructed on the site of the Bell Inn in the late nineteenth century. This photograph shows it in full use in the 1930s. At different times cattle and farm machinery sales were held there. It is now occupied by the headquarters of the Saffron Walden, Herts & Essex Building Society.

A poultry sale in the Borough Market in Hill Street. This market space was created by the Borough Council in 1831 through the purchase of the Eight Bells Inn, then on that site. The photograph was taken in the 1930s by Samuel Wenman, a bank manager and well-known amateur photographer.

A horse fair in the Market Place, 1904. They were held in March and September in the early twentieth century, but had been organised on a more or less regular basis in previous centuries. The fairs had a high reputation and attracted buyers from all over the eastern counties.

The Market Place at the end of the Tuesday market in the early years of this century. The construction of the stalls had changed little since the earliest photographs taken about fifty years before. Maynard's stall was probably that of Henry Maynard of Whittlesford, an agricultural equipment manufacturer. J.B. Pash of Chelmsford had a warehouse in Hill Street between 1936 and 1941. Other stalls belonged to James Vert, nurseryman, and Pennings, later to move into the shop seen on page 13. The photograph was taken by Underwood.

The Market Place on a busy market day in the late 1920s. William Barker also had a greengrocer's shop in Castle Street. He was a keen member of the Salvation Army. There has been a weekly market in the town since the middle ages; the right to hold a market was originally transferred to Walden from Newport in 1141. At that time it was likely to have been held on land to the west of the parish church, within the curtilage of the castle. The drinking fountain was a gift to the town made by George Stacey Gibson in 1863.

The Abbey Temperance Hotel on the corner of High Street and Abbey Lane, 1904. The Hotel was started at the suggestion of members of the Friends Meeting House and other supporters of the temperance movement. It was previously known as the Coffee Tavern. This image appeared in an advertisement published in the 'Borough' *Pocket Guide to Saffron Walden* by Edward J. Burrow.

The Market Place, looking unusually empty. This shows the shop on the right of the north-west corner under the occupancy of Joseph Scott. He was a linen draper there in 1874, before it was owned by Leverett, who in this photograph has the shop opposite, next to the Corn Exchange. This photograph was taken at about that time.

Pennings, next to the Corn Exchange in Market Place was the kind of shop many thought no longer existed. For the Penning brothers themselves, who owned it, and the thousands who patronized it through its narrow entrance, it meant an unrivalled range of groceries – not to mention a unique hand-operated 'automatic' door opening mechanism. The shop remained open until 1986, when a photographic record was made by Essex County Council.

Ruse's Mill, at the junction of Mount Pleasant Road and South Road. The mill was demolished in 1955 although it had been without sails since about 1900. The mill was unusually short, as was the nearby mill-house, which was often named the upside-down cottage, since the bedrooms were below road level and the living rooms were placed above, on the ground floor. The mill's graceful double-curved cap replaced an earlier thatched cap in about 1842.

The yard of the maltings in Gold Street. With its high, arched gateway, this is the most elegant maltings building in the town. It was associated with Day's brewery next door but one, which was demolished to make way for the Saffron Walden Laundry. The maltings are also said to have been owned by the Searles for a short time. The Searle family owned a bank in the early nineteenth century and branched out into malting, to the dismay of the Gibsons, who were maltsters of long standing. The Gibsons retaliated by opening a bank, which prospered, while both the Searle's bank and their new malting venture withered. The malting buildings have now been converted into housing, with a doctors' surgery at the rear.

The former town malt mill in the north-east corner of the Market Place. It was owned by the Borough until 1834, when it was sold to John Emson, a grocer. The peak of the gable is just visible in the upper photo on page 12, behind Emson Tanner's wholesale grocer's premises. The whole area burned down in the early 1950s and was replaced by the Emson Close group of shops.

Loading flour on to a Foden steam lorry at Holland's Mill, on the west side of Audley End Station, 1921. The mill was built there in 1896 in response to the transport and distribution needs of the forward-looking firm of Holland & Son. The original mill was on the other side of the main road and was powered by the waters of the Cam. It was taken over by Holland in 1850. The mill next to the station closed in the 1960s and the silo was eventually demolished in 1978.

Gray Palmer's shop, as it looked in about 1905 when it was already well established, having been started in Debden Road in 1887 and moved to its present site in 1895. This is one of the few instances in Saffron Walden of the same firm remaining on the same site and prospering for over 100 years. An added attraction in Christmas 1896 was a model railway 'on a rather large scale, an engine and three carriages running at a good pace over a pair of rails'.

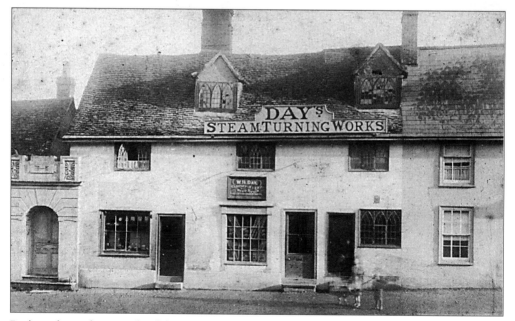

Day's works on the east side of the High Street, *c.* 1895. William Henry Day was a cabinet-maker and wood-turner. The houses are now occupied by Goddard's electrical shop. W.H. Day's business closed before 1900. Next to him was Gatward's, the watchmaker, one of whose watches is on display in the museum. The entrance to the YMCA Hall is on the extreme left. The association first met in premises in Gold Street. The hall is now used by the 1st Saffron Walden Scouts.

Cro's Market Stores in the High Street, Percy Cro and Charles Housden standing in the main entrance, *c.* 1900. This business was started in Market Hill in 1883, trading as a 'tea dealer, provision and hop merchant, Italian warehouseman, hardware dealer, agricultural implement and sewing machine agent, cabinet-maker, upholsterer, general house furnisher and furniture remover', according to a directory in 1897.

The premises of William List, boot and shoe maker, in King Street, about to be taken over by Francis John Taylor, caterer and hotel keeper, *c.* 1900. This photograph was taken by W. Frost Wilson, who took over from Hobbs in 1898.

The view along King Street before Barton's shop was enlarged in 1886. W. List's is to the left and Hardwicke's fishmonger's to the right. It is possible that this photograph was taken to record the opening of Barton's in this location, since the firm was previously listed as being only in Market Street.

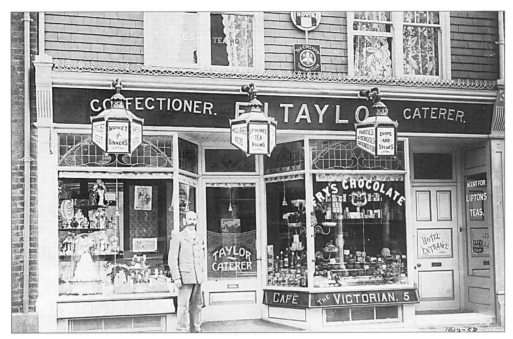

Taylor's, The Cyclists Rest and Tea Rooms. A proud Mr Taylor is standing outside the shop and hotel, so it is likely to be just after the refurbishment in 1900, started in the picture of William List opposite. Previously, The Cyclists Rest was situated in the High Street. This is now the front part of Hart's bookshop in King Street.

Barton's after the shop's enlargement, to attract more custom, in 1886. 'All classes will find it to their advantage to inspect the stock which for value and durability cannot be beaten', as a publicity flyer stated at the time. The extension is now the rear part of Hart's bookshop.

John Gilling's shop in Market Hill, *c.* 1905, when it had been on the same site for about thirty-five years. As well as being a pharmaceutical chemist he was also agent for Horniman's pure tea and 'photographic requisites'. No doubt many of the chemicals which produced the photographs in these pages were purchased in this shop. John Gilling was mayor in 1895 and 1896. This building is now occupied by the Jade Garden Chinese Restaurant.

Gilling opened a second shop in 1898 on the south side of the Market Place where it becomes King Street. The shop can also be seen in the picture on page 33, behind the drinking fountain.

King Street, *c.* 1906. Walter Robson's shop existed from about 1889 until the late 1960s. The post office was then just out of view to the right. The building which became the post office between 1920 and 1997 is just visible in the High Street. It was at that time still a private house, lived in by Dr J.P. Atkinson, mayor of the town in 1891–2, 1900–1, and 1910–16. Stead & Simpson's shop is still in the same location. One of the oldest shops that has traded continuously in the town, it was in existence on this site by 1898, and publishing catalogues of its footwear before the First World War.

The cover of Stead & Simpson's catalogue of ladies', gentlemen's and children's footwear.

Cates Corner, where Teddy Worley had the saddler's shop, 1920s. In the 1930s he moved to premises in Market Hill. The house on the opposite corner of East Street is now the Queen Elizabeth public house, which has been much enlarged. On the extreme right stood the Royal Oak, now a private house.

Worley's shop in Market Hill, 1930s. As can be seen from the notice over the garage at the back of the yard, it had previously been the Green Dragon. The licence was transferred to Sewards End, where the pub remained until it closed in 1995. As well as being a saddler, Teddy Worley made leather goods and upholstery for the motor trade, repaired bags and trunks, and, as can be seen, sold sports goods. The shop closed in about 1950; the site is now the Trustee Savings Bank.

The last location of Teddy Worley's business, in the shed in the garden of his house in Audley Road, 1970s. The workshop area at the rear of the shop in Market Hill was moved here in about 1950, and, though 'retired', Mr Worley continued mending leather goods until the late 1960s. His bench and tools are now in the museum collections.

Burton's saddlery shop in the High Street, *c.* 1914. The business existed there for about 100 years from the 1830s. It occupied the right half of a fine sixteenth-century timber-framed house, which was lived in by Wyatt George Gibson from 1817 to 1827. W.G. Gibson was a leading member of the successful malting and banking family. His son, George Stacey Gibson, was born here in 1818.

Miss Hart's woolshop on the corner of Church Street and Museum Street, *c.* 1905. Architecturally, this is the most ancient and well-preserved crossroads in the town, since the buildings on each corner date from the fifteenth century at the latest. No-one could be in any doubt where the Museum was then! The two Misses Hart formerly ran their joint business from 41 High Street.

The shops on the opposite corner of the crossroads. The Sun Inn is the most photographed building in the town, and is a complex of hall houses and gables, the earliest erected in the early fourteenth century and all replastered with elaborate pargetting designs in the seventeenth century (a number of dates adorn the façade). The nearest 'unit' was occupied in the 1880s by Whitehead & Son's china and glass stores, later Whitehead & Day, monumental masons.

Emson Tanner's wholesale grocer's business on the north side of the Market Place, decked out for the coronation of George VI in 1937. The line-up of vehicles was described by the firm as 'part of the Firm's fine fleet of motor lorries'. The business, started by John Emson, was run at this time by Ernest William Tanner, who was also a formidable local councillor between 1905 and 1927 and a JP from 1917 until the late 1930s.

The process of transformation of Emson Tanner's into Rumsey's furnishings store, 1963. It is now occupied by Eaden Lilley.

The Co-op on the corner of Gold Street and Hill Street, photographed by F.G. Davies in the 1930s. The Saffron Walden & District Co-operative Society was founded in 1901 in what had been The Bell, Castle Street, now numbers 36–8. It moved into its headquarters in the High Street (now the Capital Kebab Bar), used for grocery, drapery, boots, outfitting, furnishing and a bakery, in about 1910, with the funeral service to the rear. The Gold Street building was opened in 1929.

Thorn's shop and the Borough Market arch, just as the site was sold for development in 1983. The arch was built in 1831 to commemorate the purchase of the site to house animals in more controllable surroundings than the Market Place itself. Thorn's had earlier been owned by Jabez Gibson and was the location of the first meetings of collectors who formed themselves into the Saffron Walden Natural History Society in 1832, and founded the museum.

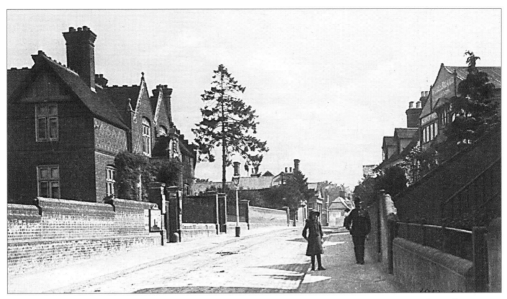

East Street, with the police station on the left, Webb & Brand's Nursery on the right, and a policeman in conversation with a girl on the pavement, *c*. 1910. The police station was built in 1886, the same year that Webb & Brand took over from Chater's the nursery buildings opposite. The firm was famous for developing double hollyhocks, surviving examples of which can still be seen in the gardens behind East Street.

Webb & Brand catalogue, autumn 1912.

The yard of Richard Atkinson Williams' livery stables in Freshwell Street, as seen in an advertisement in Burrow's booklet on the town published in about 1905, although this photograph was probably taken some five years earlier. Williams advertised himself as a Jobmaster in 1898, although the business started out by manufacturing aerated waters, initially in Bridge Street, and later on at these premises.

Advertisement for Burningham's, published in an almanac by Burrow. Although listed principally as hairdresser and fancy repository, the shop acted as agent for a number of other items as well! In Christmas 1896 he was said to display 'his customary bazaar, including mechanical and other toys, table games and a host of other amusements'.

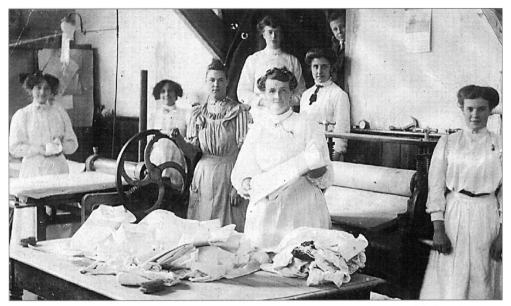

The staff of the Snowflake Laundry at work in their premises at the top of Castle Street. The laundry was started in 1907 and continued until 1968, when it was bought up by the Saffron Walden Laundry. The site had earlier been partly occupied by the Black Horse and later became the headquarters of the Salvation Army. Two houses have now been built on the site.

Delivering clean linen, *c.* 1910.

Underwood's photographer's shop, *c.* 1910. Next door a dolphin can faintly be seen in the plasterwork between the upper storey windows. This building had been a pub, the licence for which had moved from premises in King Street that were pulled down to make way for the enlarged Town Hall in 1761.

The cartouche of F.T. Day, one of the earliest professional photographers in the town. He was in business from about 1870 until about 1885 at premises in Gold Street, which were later taken over by other photographers: initially Hobbs, then Frost Wilson and afterwards Underwood.

STREETS

In the beginning there was a road, a church, a castle, a market, an abbey. As the settlement grew the streets of houses, shops and small businesses acquired the expected names: Castle Street, Church Street, Abbey Lane, Market End Street, High Street. Others were named after the occupation of their typical inhabitants: Tanner Row, Mercer Row, Butcher Row, Butter Market, Potter Row, Chesehill. Pudding Lane became Little Church Street, then Museum Street, but what of Goulstrete or Hoggs Green, Fouleslowe Lane, or Creepmouse Alley? Some acknowledged more nefarious activities: Cockpit Alley, Cuckingstole End Street, Gallows Hill. More recently there have been commemorative names of people and places, such as Winstanley Road, Old Mill Road, The Maynards. Is there ever likely to be a Tesco Mews or Waitrose Walk one wonders?

How many 'Ends' can there be to a town? There appear to have been at least five ends to Saffron Walden, although they were not all at opposite ends of the same area. There is the most famous, of course, Audley End, to the west of the town and on the edge of the parish. There are others you can find on a map: Sewards End, to the east of the parish, Bridge End, at the north end of the town. Northend formerly marked the northern extremity of the parish near Littlebury. Then there are the long-forgotten ends of the market area and the not-quite-so-long-forgotten ends of Castle Street – The City and the West End.

The view down King Street in the 1860s, showing the Town Hall built in 1761 on the left, the sign of the Hoops further down on the left, and the Corn Exchange, built in 1848, on the right. Although it is known that Youngman occupied the shop on the extreme left beside the Town Hall, there is no sign. This view would have been very different before 1761, since it would then have been possible to see the timber-framed Moot Hall blocking the entrance to King Street, with a narrow line of shops stretching behind it and the no doubt accurately named Creepmouse Alley on the left. The ghost of a policemen is just visible in the centre foreground, incompletely retouched by the unknown photographer.

Market Place and Market Street, showing the Borough Market with its arch, *c*. 1897, in the distance. It was usually called the pig market although it was never restricted to the sale of pigs. The gentlemen's toilet was built beside the arch sometime between 1898 and 1900. The toilet was demolished in 1984 when Waitrose was built, but the arch was incorporated into the new structure. Thompson's stationers, beside the Town Hall, operated between 1896 and 1914.

Market Hill, looking towards the Church Street junction, with Isaac Marking's butcher's shop visible on the far corner. The Green Dragon on the left remained there until Teddy Worley took it over as a saddlery shop in the 1930s. Below the sign for Rowntree's chocolates and pastilles on the other side of the road is a poster advertising the coming of 'The Pirates' and 'The Green Eye of the Yellow God' to the Walden Cinema (which can be seen on page 56).

Church Path, leading up to the parish church, with Dorset House on the right. The headquarters of the Territorials before the Second World War, it was demolished in 1958. The plaster was removed from the row of houses on the left during 1958. The railings at the end were removed early in the 1940s, supposedly to help the war effort.

The junction of Castle Street and Museum Street, earlier called Little Church Street, and in the seventeenth century Pudding Lane. This is the area that the stocks and the market cross were moved to from the Market Place when it was spruced up in 1819. The Castle continued as an inn until 1974. The sign for the Five Bells is just visible further down the street. The Reed family still runs the antique shop in the property on the extreme left.

Bridge Street, *c.* 1910: another composition with posed figures by Underwood. The Victorian post box on the corner is the one shown on page 74. It was later moved to the other side of Castle Street, set within its own brick column, and is now on display in the museum. The earliest allotments in the town can be seen beyond the houses in the distance.

Bridge Street, looking south from the bridge over the Madgate Slade, with the sixteenth-century Eight Bells pub on the left. Note the distinctive linked Tudor chimneys on the right, also seen in the illustration of the backs of these low-lying houses on page 76.

View from the top of the High Street. The house on the left at the top is very similar today, but the street itself looks different because of the London plane trees, planted in 1902. The building at the bottom of the hill on the right, with the cart in front, is the Greyhound, before the gable on George Street was removed in about 1875. The presence of this gable narrowed the entrance into George Street to about 10 feet.

The High Street in the early morning, with everybody posing, even at the top of the street, *c.* 1912. The milkman is outside the Greyhound delivering milk from churns. On the right, with the columned portico, is another property owned by the Gibson family, this one by Wyatt George Gibson after he moved out of the house further up the High Street in 1827. This photograph was taken by Underwood.

The High Street to the north in about 1900, before The Cyclists Rest had moved to King Street. The Cross Keys shows the crossed keys in a cartouche designed by Selena Pitstow before the timbers were exposed in 1910, as seen on page 67. The shop covered in posters on the opposite corner was replaced by the present building in 1908.

Gold Street looking north in about 1900, soon after the Castle Brewery ceased operating, but before the Saffron Walden Laundry business was well established. Day's funeral business started in the house next door; it was later inherited by the Peasgoods. The building has just been reconverted into a family home.

The entrance to one of the many yards in the town, photographed by Newland Talbot, 1904. This one in King Street gave access to the Tailors Arms in the nineteenth century and probably other inns in earlier times; the timber-work is sixteenth century in origin, and some very fine carved beams were found when the shop to the left was renovated in 1906. The poster on the right advertises Cassell's Magazine with the caption 'The Navy of Japan'. One beside it lampoons the Masons. This was the way through to Hart's printing works. (See also the picture on page 109.)

Houses on Common Hill on the western side of the Common, including The Priory with the tall chimney and Whitehead & Day's monumental mason's premises on the right, with the stone slabs in front. Between the two, in front of the parish church tower and spire, is the cowl of the maltings in what is now Emson Close. The Priory was at one time a school, run by the Misses Day. The folly to the left of The Priory is clearly visible; this has since gone. This postcard was sent in May 1930, but the image dates from the mid-1920s.

Common Hill, c. 1920. Note the tombstones for sale at Whitehead & Day's premises, caught by the early morning sun. The noticeboard was put up by the Saffron Walden Sanitary Authority, and concerns the prohibition on the beating of carpets. This photograph was taken by Underwood and shows his characteristic style: compare it with the image of Bridge Street on page 35 – the similar clarity of light, the same time of day and the familiar posed figures.

A view over the town from the Friends School, when it was new in 1879. The open space was soon to be filled with large town villas, seen in the photograph opposite. The railway line was opened in 1868. The station platforms and the Railway Tavern can be seen on the right, partially obscured by the pair of newly built semi-detached houses in West Road.

Station Street from one of the newly built houses on West Road, 1880s. Graded piles of coal lie in the sidings area in the foreground, now partly occupied by flats built in 1994. Although the houses on the far side look as if they were built as a result of the railway, they were built before it came, in 1856 as the dates on the fronts indicate.

Mount Pleasant Road at the junction with Debden Road, *c.* 1905, showing the villas built in the 1880s. This postcard was sent on 12 November 1909 with a half-penny stamp.

South Road, when the villas on the west side were new, and before any pavements were laid down, *c.* 1900. The houses show good examples of patterned brickwork.

The corner of East Street and Fairycroft Road, *c.* 1904. This was photographed just before the demolition of the house in the middle to widen the opening to the road formerly known as Foundry Lane. (See page 22 for a picture of the junction after the house was taken away.) The Royal Oak ceased to be a pub in about 1910. The Queen Elizabeth, on the far corner, was said to be a pub at that time; although there is no sign to indicate this, the notice above the glazed door mentions Timothy Hunt, the publican.

Artisans' dwellings erected in 1882 by Dix, Green & Co., cement manufacturers of West Road, to house their workmen. They were built with concrete supplied from the factory.

The Street, Audley End village, with the post office on the left, *c.* 1895. Apart from cars instead of the pony and trap, the scene in 1997 has changed little.

The other end of the village street, about ten years later, playing host to a school visit. This scene was captured by Skelton, an amateur photographer.

The Fulfen Slade stream at the end of Audley End village, *c.* 1895. The efficiency of using a yoke to carry pails is clearly demonstrated.

PUBLIC BUILDINGS

In the more distant past, buildings for public use in general or for the specific use of certain categories of people in the town in particular, were usually constructed for the glorification of the individuals who paid to have them built. Although the parish church was initially a humble structure for the worship of God, the subsequent additions and embellishments were erected to the greater glory of the benefactors. Geoffrey de Mandeville gave money for a priory to be built (later to become Walden Abbey) to provide space for monks to pray for his everlasting deliverance.

More recently motives have been less self-serving. Mary Gibson bought the land in Hill Street so that public swimming baths could be built on it, although in 1985 very few people knew of this when this valuable town centre area was sold for shopping development. The Boys British School building and the Training College are other examples of Gibson generosity. The Corn Exchange was built by the Borough with some private finance, and was in 1973 taken over by the County Council for more obvious public benefit. The museum building was erected in 1834 by Lord Braybrooke for the use of various local societies in which he had an interest. A combination of public money, public-spiritedness by some individuals and enlightened self-interest by others has resulted in a range of buildings for public use which few small towns elsewhere can offer. A major regret is that there is no longer a cinema here, where once there were two!

One of the earliest photographs of the town, taken between 1852 and 1854 (presumably by J.M. Youngman), of the new Corn Exchange, built in 1848. On the extreme right is Leverett's drapery shop, which was demolished in 1854 or 1855. The notice above the doorway refers to the Royal Exchange Assurance Fire & Life Office. Youngman's shop was on the diagonally opposite corner of the Market Place beside the town hall where this photograph was taken. Note the cobbled paving and the absence of kerbs.

The Woolcombers' Hall, which was demolished in 1848 to make way for the Corn Exchange. Unfortunately, apart from this drawing (made in 1848 partially as a conjectural reconstruction, and published in *The Builder*), this remarkable hall was not recorded in detail before it was taken down.

The Town Hall as it appeared before the addition of the mock Tudor façade in 1879, photographed by W. Hobbs. The ground floor area had been used as a lock-up until 1818. Boardman took over the shop to the left of the Town Hall from Youngman in 1875.

The enlarged Town Hall, c. 1900.

The post office range of buildings, erected in 1889 in King Street, from a contemporary print. The post office first operated from a building on the site of the Corn Exchange, then from within the Scientific and Literary Institution until 1876, when it moved into offices in Market Hill. It moved into these purpose-built offices in King Street in 1889, then finally to the High Street in 1920. This building is now occupied by W.H. Smiths, with the Oxfam shop, Stead & Simpson and New Look to the left.

Barclays Bank and the Rose & Crown in the Market Place. The bank was built in 1874 for Gibson, Tuke & Gibson by W. Eden Nesfield, who also restored the façade of the Rose & Crown. It remained the premier coaching inn for the town until a tragic fire on Boxing Day 1969 caused the death of eleven guests. The ruined building was pulled down, although the façade was still standing. The new building is now Boots the Chemists. The bunch of grapes has been positioned on its front, and the canopy over the front entrance has been inserted in a rear wall of the new building. This photograph was taken by Simpson Bros of Cambridge probably in 1879, soon after the bank first opened.

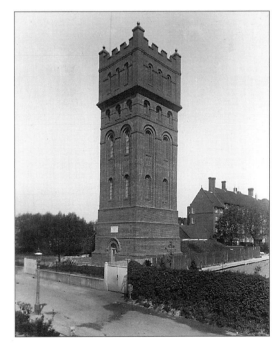

The water tower in Debden Road, built in 1913 to cater for new housing to the south of the town. The first deep bore hole for water was dug in the centre of the town to a depth of 1,000 feet in 1836, at the instigation of Jabez Gibson who was concerned to provide clean water for the town. The Saffron Walden Water Company was founded in 1862, and a new borehole was dug in 1899. This water tower became redundant in the 1960s and was replaced by the concrete tower on the Thaxted Road in 1966. The tower was bought by the Friends School, seen on the right of the picture, and remains as the dominant landmark on the southern side of town. The photograph was taken by Underwood.

Swimming Baths in Hill Street, built in 1910. The site was given by Miss Gibson, G.S. Gibson's daughter. The men's changing area was at the side. It was unheated; in the winter this made the water seem warm, but getting out and changing was a torture. The Slade stream ran underneath the baths in a culvert, which was declared unsafe in 1982. The baths were demolished in 1984 to make way for the present shopping development. This photograph was taken soon after the baths opened.

The General Hospital, built in 1866, using a bequest of £5,000 from Wyatt George Gibson on land donated by Lord Braybrooke. The building was designed by William Beck. Additions were made to the building in 1925 and 1935; these were removed when the hospital was converted into the headquarters of Uttlesford District Council in 1990. This photograph was taken in the early years of the twentieth century.

Engraving of the Gas Works in Thaxted Road, built in 1836. The guiding lights in this enterprise were Jabez Gibson and John Player, both of whom wished to improve living conditions in the town by providing street lighting. The buildings still exist, although the urn-topped chimneys have long since disappeared. The drawing is by John Mallows Youngman.

The town's railway station was built in 1868. It was on the branch line from Audley End main line station to Ashdon and Bartlow. The line was the first to be closed by the Beeching cuts in 1963. The track was taken up almost immediately and the area is now occupied by Cleales Garage, but the station building, minus the awning, and the Railway Tavern are still there.

These almshouses in Park Lane, built in 1782, replaced earlier tenements put up in 1400 originally to provide a 'house of charity for the succour and sustenance of 13 poor men'. It was cheerless accommodation, according to Lord Braybrooke, writing in 1834, but the houses were not replaced until 1950 when Primes Close was built, using a bequest from the Revd Joseph Prime.

Gibson Free Dwellings, built in Abbey Lane in 1840 for ex-employees of the family, presumably both from the bank and from the various Gibson houses in the town. In 1950 they were placed under the control of the Almshouse Trustees. The buildings were sold in 1980 and are now privately owned. This photograph was taken in about 1910 by Underwood.

The College of St Mark in Audley End village. This sixteenth-century building is thought originally to have been a hospital attached to Walden Abbey, and later used as almshouses. The building still has the appearance of almshouses, erected around two courtyards (male and female?), each with a well and with a shared chapel. It was taken over by the Diocese of Chelmsford, originally as housing for retired clergy and more recently as a residential educational centre for young people.

The ornately carved mantelpiece of the kitchen in the College of St Mark, before 1905.

A view of the town showing the parish church before the spire was added in 1832. The lantern on top of the tower was said to have been designed by Henry Winstanley in the 1680s and used by him as the model for the top most part of the first lighthouse on the Eddystone rocks, which he designed in 1696. This print, dated 1831, also shows how dominant Dorset House was in Church Street, immediately below the church tower. Dorset House can be seen in the photograph of Church Path on page 34.

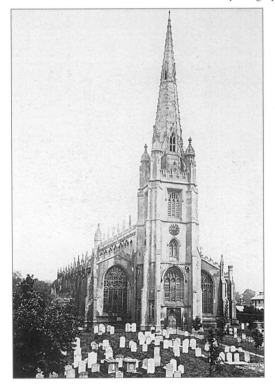

The parish church St Mary the Virgin with spire, designed by Rickman and added in 1832. This photograph was taken by A. Seeley of Richmond Hill, Surrey, in about 1876. It shows the gravestones in place in the churchyard, and the avenue of huge plane trees lining the path down to the High Street as saplings.

Interior view of the parish church, photographed by F.T. Day before 1875. Towards the end of the century the chairs were replaced by oak pews. The rood screen was added in 1923 and the rood itself in 1952; both were donated by William Favill Tuke, connected by marriage to the Gibson family and at one time chairman of Barclays Bank. The font now stands in the south aisle.

The interior of the Abbey Lane Congregational Chapel, now the United Reform Church, 1905. It was built in 1811. The first Independent Meeting House was a barn in Abbey Lane, replaced by a chapel ready for use in 1694.

The Baptist Church, built in 1879 in front of the original chapel, which had been built in 1774. The lamp-post at the top of the High Street was the one originally erected in the centre of the Market Place, soon after the town gas supply was initiated in 1836. It was moved to this position in 1862 when the drinking fountain was placed in the centre of the Market Place. The lamp-post was moved again, to its present position on the south side of the junction, when the war memorial was put in its place in 1921. The cinema was built in 1912, burnt down and rebuilt in 1950 and finally closed and demolished in 1973. This photograph was taken by Underwood.

The church hall of the United Reform Church, originally built as a school belonging to the Congregational Chapel in 1836.

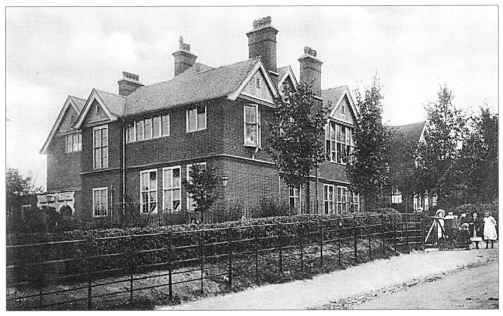

The Practising School in South Road, with children outside the front entrance, 1910. Later it became known as the South Road School. From its opening in 1902 it was attached to the Teacher Training College. The College had been built in 1884 with money supplied by George Stacey Gibson. It was closed in 1978, and taken over by the Bell Educational Trust as an English language teaching centre.

The entrance to the old Grammar School in Castle Street, behind Walsingham House, 1919. The inscription may date from 1655: translated it reads 'either learn, teach or leave'. The Grammar School was founded in 1525. After many changes of fortune it moved into new premises in Ashdon Road in 1881, now occupied by Dame Bradbury's Preparatory School. This photograph was taken by Samuel Wenman.

Dame Bradbury's school building, when it was the Grammar School, 1905. It was built through the combined generosity of Lord Braybrooke and George Stacey Gibson. During the latter part of the Second World War it was used as the headquarters of the United States Army Air Force 65th Fighter Wing.

Pupils in the playground of the Friends School, and a master with a penny-farthing bicycle. The Preparatory School is on the left. This is one of a number of official photographs taken by Bedford Lemaire, of The Strand, London, when the school was first opened in 1879.

Boys and girls at the Preparatory School for the Friends School, 1879.

Saffron Walden Museum, 1890. The curator of the time, George Nathan Maynard, and his wife are standing either side of the iron railings. The building was erected at the behest of Lord Braybrooke, who owned the site, in 1834, partly to house the collections of the Saffron Walden Natural History Society on the first floor in the left-hand half, and partly as meeting rooms for other organisations. The Agricultural Society held its meetings and its annual dinner in the long room on the right, which was consequently called the Agricultural Hall. When the Town Hall was enlarged in 1879, the Agricultural Hall became redundant as a meeting venue. The whole building was then taken over as a museum, with G.N. Maynard as its first paid curator, although Joseph Clarke, who had been honorary curator for many years, continued to have his room in the museum until he died in 1895.

The entrance hall to the museum in about 1910 showing, amongst other things, one of the elaborately carved mantelpieces made of 'clunch'. These were formerly in the house lived in during the sixteenth century by the Harvey family, and which later became The Bell. It was demolished in 1852 to make way for the cattle market seen on page 10.

The interior of the museum, *c*. 1910. This is a section of the ethnographical room, including Asian weapons and steel dishes, a model of an East African Arab dhow above the showcase and Australian aboriginal artefacts on the back wall. The museum has been through a number of refurbishments since then, but many of the Australian objects can still be seen in the 'Worlds of Man' gallery.

The interior of the ruined keep of Walden Castle, originally built in about 1141 and partially demolished in about 1158. The museum building was built in the grounds of the castle in 1834, and in the early years of this century the ruined keep housed some museum objects. The medieval stone coffins are from the priories at Ickleton and Berden, two nearby villages. The pillory is from the lock-up at Newport on the old toll road to Newmarket.

The entrance to Bridge End Garden and the Gibson Gallery in Castle Street, *c.* 1920. This gallery housed a number of old masters, as well as local watercolours, collected by Francis Gibson from 1830 until his death in 1859. It existed in this form until 1970 and re-emerged in the spring of 1987 as the Fry Art Gallery, concentrating on twentieth-century artists working in north-west Essex.

The Scientific and Literary Institution in King Street. This Institution (later known by the less threatening name 'Institute') was founded in 1832, at the same time as the Saffron Walden Natural History Society. The building it now occupies was built at the same time as the Corn Exchange, in 1848. The librarian lived in the house on the left. Today, the children's library is on the ground floor of the building, the Town Library above, and the County Library in the former Corn Exchange, bought and converted for the purpose in the early 1970s.

A photograph from the front page of a publicity brochure published in about 1930, showing the first floor reading room. The brochure states that the librarian will be found 'at his residence at any time' other than when the library is open – days off were clearly out of the question!

The Duke of York pub at the top of the High Street; it has been a pub for over 120 years. This photograph shows that it was run by Hawkes & Son, with Julius Green as publican. Next to the pub in Debden Road there had been a famous bone wall, about 7 feet high and 200 yards long, composed entirely of the fore-parts of the crania of oxen, secured to the bank behind the wall with the horns. It was built up in the eighteenth century, and had disappeared by about 1820.

The fireplace in the parlour of the Greyhound, with iron basket grate, seventeenth-century wrought-iron crane, kettle and beer-warmer. Samuel Wenman took this photograph in 1926.

PRIVATE HOUSES
& BUILDING STYLES

In a town like Saffron Walden, with such a wealth of housing traditions from different centuries and so much evidence to examine the way they have changed, it is fascinating to plot how tastes in the way houses look have altered. In the fifteenth century a heavily timbered appearance was in favour, for those who could afford it. In the sixteenth and seventeenth centuries, as good straight oak beams became more scarce and more expensive, new timbered buildings were less elegant to view and were more often covered in plaster. In this part of East Anglia, the plaster was often highly decorated, in relief on the outside through pargetting, and by painting patterns in panels on the inside. The really wealthy built in stone of course, but with little suitable building stone available locally, they also had to bear the cost of haulage. Lord Howard de Walden could certainly afford to build Audley End House in stone, using the ruins of Walden Abbey as foundations, but even here much of the façade was built of clunch, an inferior local stone.

When an existing timber-framed structure was sound but old-fashioned, the most effective face-lift was to refront the building in brick. As bricks became cheaper in the seventeenth century they were used more frequently, first the warm old soft reds, then the harder, yellow/white gault bricks. In the Victorian period, as the technology of controlling kiln temperatures progressed and bricks of different colours could be produced, patterns in brickwork became the order of the day. Earlier in the present century it became fashionable to remove added plaster from timber-framed houses, even when this was not warranted by the quality of the original! Meanwhile new technology and materials appear, cement, concrete, steel, glass cladding, all creating their own typical forms. And the reversion to earlier styles, or rather pastiches of them is not new – late twentieth-century houses may have Georgian-style windows and doors, but even the nineteenth-century Town Hall is mock-Tudor!

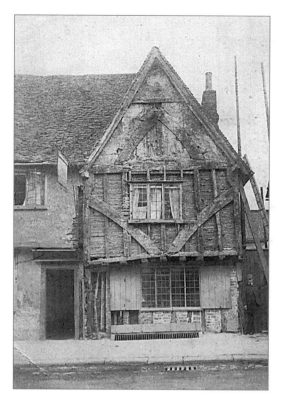

The Greyhound pub at the bottom of High Street, now the offices of the *Cambridge Evening News*, at the time the plaster was being stripped off in 1888, showing the fine braces on the gabled front. The photograph was taken by Hobbs.

The gable on the eastern wing of the medieval hall house on the corner of King Street and Cross Street, while the building was being renovated, not long after the side of the building was re-rendered in 1906. The removal of the rendering revealed sixteenth-century windows which were reinstated, the later sash windows being removed. The restoration work was supervised by Guy Maynard, the curator of the museum. He, therefore, was presumably responsible for the insertion of the trefoil heads to the windows, similar to the ones put in the High Street façade of the Cross Keys, and taken from an example in the museum. The whole range of shops and the house, from the corner to Williams the optician's, was originally built as a single large house in the fifteenth century, the ground floor of the part in this picture then being used as a shop.

The Cross Keys on the corner of High Street and King Street, just after the rendering was removed and the timbering renovated, 1920. The picture on page 37 of the High Street shows the inn before the work was done. The large sash windows on the King Street façade have been removed to allow the fifteenth-century windows to be re-used. The changes to the High Street façade are more interesting, especially the trefoil headings inserted in the plastered panels either side of the first floor window and the zig-zag bracing below the window, both features thought to be original by subsequent generations. The earliest evidence from the timbers on this building suggests it was erected in about 1375.

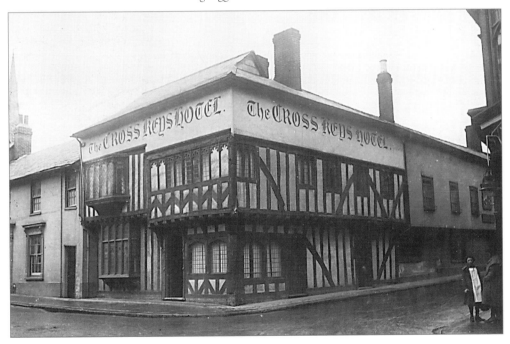

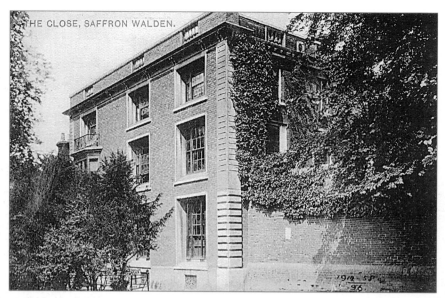

The house that moved. This was in the High Street, part of The Close, the house with the spider window which is still on the corner of Castle Street. The brick façade added in 1854 by Francis Gibson conceals a timber frame. The re-fronted building was sold in 1934, dismantled and re-erected in West Grinstead, and called Walden Close. When the house was being stripped, seventeenth-century wall paintings and a fragment of the twelfth-century market cross were discovered. The fragment of the stone cross, seen in the photograph opposite, went with the house to Sussex.

The exposed frame just before it was taken down and moved, but after the internal plaster had been removed. The remaining part of the house on the left was divested of its rendering later in the 1930s, and the ground floor wall at the front, with the spider window, was taken away to reveal the original stud-work wall, jettied at first floor level. The front door and spider window were re-positioned and the window rebuilt at a slightly different height.

The Close as it appears today. Like many ancient timber-framed houses in the town, it has survived many changes. Originally built early in the fifteenth century, it was owned by the Baron family in the seventeenth century, and by John Strachey, a pioneer student of geology, in the early eighteenth century. The complete house was bought by Francis Gibson in the 1830s. In the later nineteenth century it was used as a convent, the corner gabled wing housing the chapel.

The section of the twelfth-century market cross found supporting one of the wall plates at the front of the house. Another fragment of the same cross is set into the exterior east wall of the south porch of the parish church. It is thought that the cross was set up in the area between the church and the High Street before the churchyard existed there, when the market was held in this area.

Houses in the High Street, formerly weavers' cottages with typical high windows to light their work, but now Evans Army & Navy Stores, replastered with pargetting designs in the 1920s.

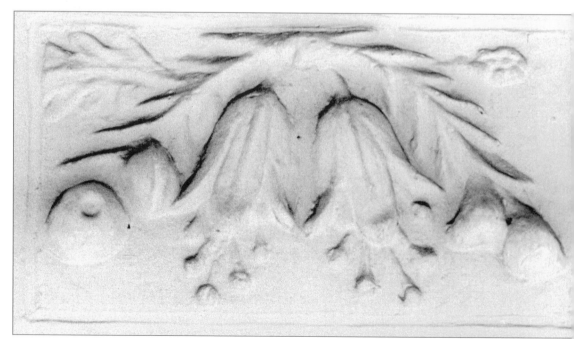

One of the pargetting designs used on this house. A somewhat inaccurate version of the saffron crocus is the floral part of the design.

The back of Myddylton House in the corner of Myddylton Place. It was said to have been formerly called Hoggs Green House, since the area was once known as Hoggs Green; however, the late Cliff Stacey, one-time town clerk and expert on the history of the town, has argued that Hoggs Green House was a different building nearby, pulled down in about 1758. The magnificent mantelpiece seen in the photograph below was apparently moved from the earlier house 'next door' into the ground floor room of this house, to the right of the porch.

The mantelpiece in Myddylton House. The carving depicts a barrel or 'tun' flanked by 'myd' and 'dyl' hence the pun. The carved timber of the mantelpiece was originally in the home of the Myddylton family, Hoggs Green House. The photograph was taken by Walter Francis, an amateur photographer, at the end of the nineteenth century.

The house and shop formerly occupying the site of the old post office and shops in King Street seen on page 48. This building was demolished in 1888.

Houses on the east side of the High Street, c. 1900, just before the plane trees were planted in 1902. The gabled house on the right was the premises of John Hughes, a coachbuilder. Like a number of timber-framed houses in the High Street, the building was refaced in brick — in this case after a fire in 1912. It is now occupied by Walden Motors, and although the ground floor showroom frontage is quite different, the gables are still visible above it.

Two cottages in Museum Street, demolished in 1894 to provide recreation space for the infants in the school just visible on the left of the picture. The school building is now used by the museum as a teaching area and laboratory. The playground site has now been filled with a new residence called Pudding House, commemorating the time when this street was known as Pudding Lane in the earlier eighteenth century.

The house on the corner of Myddylton Place and Bridge Street, now a Youth Hostel. Like The Close, diagonally opposite this house, it was originally built in the early fifteenth century as a merchant's house, with a number of fine decorative external features. Examples are the dragon post on the corner carved with falling drapery (below the gas lamp) and the oriel windows on the first floor, above the cart. By the end of the sixteenth century at least, the back part of the house had been converted into a maltings, hence the housing in the roof for the sack hoist. It was still being put to the same use when this photograph was taken during the First World War. The soldier is posting a letter in the box on the opposite corner visible in the picture on page 35; perhaps he was a patient at Walden Place, at the further end of Myddylton Place? (See the illustrations on pages 100 and 101.)

The same building, after it had ceased to be a maltings and had been taken over by the Ancient Buildings Trust. In the manner that was becoming common, the section of the building on the corner had been renovated by the removal of plaster and exposure of the very fine timber framing. The schoolchildren posing in front were not staying here since the building did not become a Youth Hostel until 1942. They may be pupils of the Friends School, since the photograph was taken by C.B. Rowntree, the deputy headmaster, in August 1932.

Part of School Row and 93 Castle Street, demolished in the 1930s as part of the slum clearance operation.

House and shop in the High Street in 1912, numbers 52 and 54, lived in at that time by Frank Clayden and James Costin respectively. In the 1930s both parts were bought up by Cole's for use as the retail outlet for their bakery business. The right-hand shop is now occupied by the offices of the *Saffron Walden Reporter*. The arch at the entrance to the YMCA Hall, now used by the 1st Saffron Walden Scout Group, encroaches on the shops on either side.

Houses on the bend of Myddylton Place before being smartened up in the 1930s.

The backs of houses in Bridge Street, low-lying and damp, in an area of the town that often flooded at this time, 1922. This photograph gives a good indication of the kind of conditions endured by most people living in this part of the town until the 1950s.

St Aylotts farmhouse, on the extreme eastern edge of Saffron Walden parish on the road to Ashdon. This is an outstanding moated house, built in the mid-fifteenth century on a rectangular plan, with a great hall and wings to north and south; internal evidence for this remains. It is a Grade I listed building, although it might not look it in this photograph taken in the 1930s.

The barn of St Aylotts farmhouse, 1930s. It was demolished in the 1960s as it was the wrong size and shape to accommodate modern farm machinery, and no longer needed to store or deal with farm produce. This was shortly before the time when such structures were valued as the architectural masterpieces they are now recognised to be. The huge barn doors, designed to allow access for farm carts and for a through draught to help thresh the corn when it was winnowed by hand, were falling off their hinges.

The Great Hall of Audley End House when being used as a private house by Lord Braybrooke, *c.* 1900. The walls are decorated with paintings of members of the family and trophies, including the usual Indian shields and spears. The most impressive feature is the magnificent seventeenth-century carved oak screen. The fireplace, although enlarged from the original seventeenth-century hearth, still seems ridiculously small for such a huge and opulently furnished room.

The north and south wings on the eastern side of Audley End House. These follow the line of the cloisters of Walden Abbey, demolished in 1538–9. This photograph was taken by A. Seeley in about 1895.

OPEN SPACES

The Common has for centuries been the largest piece of open space in the town, although strictly speaking it was never common land. One of the earliest references to a leisure event was the licensing of a fair. There is a report of a thirteenth-century joust within the land of the castle, which ended in tragedy when the event was used to settle a private score between two contestants. The gardens of large houses have given most of the town a leafy air, but there were nevertheless areas of high density and poor-quality housing, in Castle Street in particular, in the nineteenth century. This made access to the nearby open spaces a necessity rather than a luxury, for hanging out washing and beating carpets, despite official injunctions.

In the present century, Bridge End Gardens, Jubilee Gardens, the Battle Ditches, the Anglo-American Playing Fields, and other playing fields in the town have combined to give every neighbourhood access to some form of play and recreation space. The nearby farm land, roadways and footpaths around the town have also been well used for walks, for example along Seven Devils Lane and the walk through Westley Farm.

Nevertheless some open spaces have been lost as areas of comparative wildness in the generally neat urban landscape – Swan Meadow being the latest and most bitterly fought example.

Sledging on the Common, showing the brushwood fence that protected the area of the cricket pitch in winter, *c.* 1904. The land in the background on Ashdon Road had not then been used as the site for the Carmelite Convent, which was built in 1927–8 and used for about fifty years before being sold to make way for De Bohun Court. This picture was taken by Newland Talbot.

The Common looking west, *c.* 1910. The tent belonged to Harold Woodward, who held sales of farm vehicles and machinery on the top corner of the Common, beneath the trees on the right of the picture.

Drawing of the turf maze. The first mention of this medieval maze occurred in 1699, when it was re-cut. Tradition relates that it is a smaller copy of one further east, but there is no evidence for this. This drawing shows it as it was in 1858, when it was disparagingly said to be a playground for children. Formerly there was an ash tree in the centre; this was said to have been burnt down during a Guy Fawkes celebration

The turf maze on the Common, 1990. The walking line of the maze was originally defined by the removal of turf, but was reinforced by the insertion of bricks, first put in on edge in 1911 then laid flat in 1979. This is the largest maze of this type in the country. It has been re-cut many times, including in about 1818 when local tradesman John Leverett raised a subscription for this to be done.

Beechy Rye, which follows the line of the
Fulfen Slade between Audley End Road and
Newport Road, *c.* 1930. This is a favourite
walking haunt for Walden people. The
photograph was taken by Samuel Wenman.

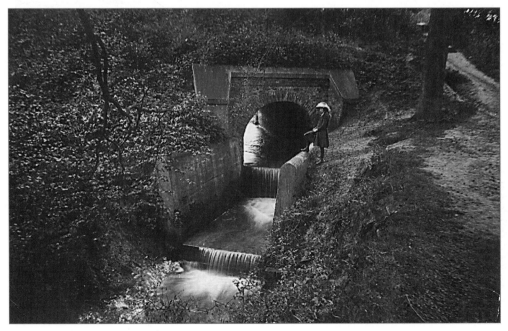

The Fulfen Slade stream, culverted as it flows under Newport Road and through Beechy Rye. The
photograph was taken by Underwood in about 1912, and this postcard was sent on 3 January 1915.

Debden Road as it curves round by the pond in front of Roos Farm, at the junction with the green lane leading to Thaxted Road, *c.* 1900. This lane was formerly the location of the medieval village of Thunderley, stricken and deserted at the time of the great plagues in the fourteenth century. This photograph was taken by Walter Francis.

Looking towards the town from the road to Ashdon, 1915. The water tower by the Friends School can be seen on the left, the long low building in the centre distance is the Union Workhouse, later known as St James's and now the Saffron Walden Community Hospital. The photograph was taken by Samuel Wenman.

Bridge End Gardens were laid out by Atkinson Francis Gibson in the 1830s. They became the principal interest of Francis Gibson, one of his sons, who laid out a large area, including the formal Dutch Garden shown here, a rose garden and a hedge maze, and also had a summerhouse built. The figure supporting the fountain in the middle of the pond has recently been discovered to be a triton by John van Nost, a London sculptor working between 1695 and 1710.

Bridge End Gardens, after a gale brought down one of the large cedars of Lebanon, 1930. See the photographs on page 105 for a view of the tree in its heyday. Samuel Wenman took the photograph.

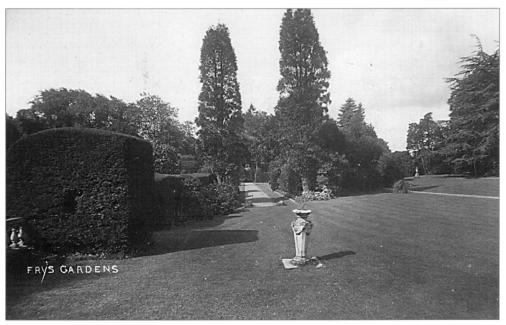

The Gardens are also known as Fry's Gardens because they were, and still are, owned by the Fry family. Francis Gibson's daughter Elizabeth married Sir Lewis Fry of Bristol. This view shows the sundial and the path to the summerhouse, and was photographed by Underwood in about 1912.

Two views of the Iron Age hill fort in the grounds of Audley End Estate. This is now deep in woodland and inaccessible, but when these photographs were taken by Skelton between 1920 and 1930 the undergrowth had been chopped away to reveal the considerable bank and ditch arrangement, known as Ring Hill. The fort was positioned on the western bank of the Cam valley to control access along the valley in the centuries before the coming of the Romans.

The south-west corner of the so-called 'Battle Ditches', with the London Road hospital in the background. These ditches were cut in the late thirteenth century supposedly to define the boundary of the new town which was being laid out at that time. There was never a battle connected with these earthworks; at the time of construction it was just called *magnum fossatum* or great ditch. One theory is that they were cut to improve drainage in the High Street; dug sufficiently deep to cater for the rain water run-off from the ducking pond at the top of the High Street, and so preventing the excess water cascading down the street during wet weather.

Part of the excavations in the garden of 53 High Street, a Gibson family property, now part of the Gibson Gardens estate. The dig was supervised by G.S. Gibson, and uncovered over 200 human remains, some associated with the Roman period but most of them with the Saxon village of Waledana. Also found in the cemetery was a superb Viking necklace now in the museum. Note the Abbey Lane United Reform Church in the background, the interior of which is shown on page 56.

The excavation of the Romano/British and Saxon cemetery, 1876. The science and procedures of archaeology were then in their infancy. Although these diggers appear to be taking a somewhat cavalier attitude to the bodies surrounding them, the skeletons themselves seem to have been exposed with great care. The whole excavation was reasonably well recorded for such an early date, although much more data would be obtained if such an excavation were to be undertaken today. After recording, a small number of the skeletons were removed, three to the town museum, some others to the Ashmolean Museum in Oxford. The rest were re-interred.

The garden to Hill House, the large town house at the top of the High Street, occupied by members of the Gibson family. This photograph dates from the 1920s when Miss Gibson lived there. Her father, George Stacey Gibson, lived there until his death in 1883. He was the author of the first *Flora of Essex*, which was the standard work on local botany until the 1970s. When Miss Gibson died, the garden was sold for housing. The area is now occupied by part of the Gibson Gardens estate.

The tent of F.T. Day, 'Photographic Artist', with several people posing in front of it at the Essex Agricultural Show, held in the Deer Park of Audley End House, probably in 1884. The tent on the left advertises 'Wash and Brush Up', but no-one appears to be taking advantage of its facilities!

Abbey Lane, viewed from the entrance to Audley Park looking in the direction of the almshouses, c. 1905. This road connected the town with Walden Abbey between the twelfth and sixteenth centuries, but is much older than that since it follows the line of an east–west track in existence during the Roman occupation.

A fine specimen of a bull, one of many that were kept in the castle meadow in front of the museum by Isaac Marking before going to his slaughterhouse in Museum Street. The proprietorial grin below the homburg belongs to Hubert Collar, museum curator between 1920 and 1948.

The allotments on Windmill Hill, being worked by the mayor, Dr Atkinson, as part of the war effort between 1914 and 1918. These were among the earliest allotments in the town.

EVENTS & ACTIVITIES

A caption on one photograph in the museum collection says 'a sleepy town, nothing goes on here' and the old railwayman's label for the town was 'God help you'. While the young refer to 'suffering boredom' this is hardly the opinion you would get from anyone during carnival time or from any member of one of the hundreds of clubs and societies in the town.

From the days of jousting in the thirteenth century to the fairs on the Common and the annual Guy Fawkes celebration there is no shortage of things to do, although inevitably not enough to please every taste.

Although there is no uniquely Waldenian event to match Thaxted's morris ring or Dunmow's flitch trial, there was formerly a festival to celebrate Bishop Blaize, the patron saint of woolcombers who had an important role to play in finishing woollen cloth. This consisted of a parade and a special anthem.

A similar book being compiled in 100 years' time will doubtless contain pictures of revellers at the Saffron Walden Folk Festival, which has established itself as an outstanding programme of events in a very short time.

The High Street at the time of Queen Victoria's silver jubilee, when this flower arch was built over the roadway, 1862. A similar one was built in London Road, outside the house called Larchmount.

During the 1860s George Stacey Gibson's garden to Hill House at the top of the High Street must have been one of the most splendid to visit in the town, especially when the Floral Fête was being held. (See the photograph of part of the garden on page 88.) His was not only one of the largest gardens in the town, but no doubt the most interesting for the horticulturally minded, as he was the author of the *Flora of Essex*, published in 1862.

The proclamation of Edward VII's accession to the throne in 1901, made at the top of the High Street in the presence of the mayor, Dr J.P. Atkinson, in chain and white gloves. He is standing on the steps in front of the door facing down the High Street.

The Market Place during the 1902 coronation. All the stops were pulled out for the celebration since there had not been a coronation for sixty-four years. There were strings of roses suspended from a central pole, just visible on the extreme left of this photograph, and the crown on the façade of the Town Hall was illuminated with gas jets. Presumably the perishable decorations would have had to be renewed, as the coronation itself was delayed at the last minute owing to the continuing illness of the King.

The top of the High Street also bedecked for the same occasion. A pole was erected where the war memorial is now, with bunting down both sides of the street. Note the newly planted plane trees in their protective iron grilles. These were given by Edmund Birch Gibson and planted in March 1902.

The next coronation, in June 1911, was an equally lavish affair. Here is an official element of it, the mayoral procession at the bottom of Church Street turning into the High Street. Town Clerk William Adams, in the wig, precedes the Sergeant at Arms and the Mace-bearer, Charles William Charter.

A dinner was given for all those in the town who were eligible to receive the new pension, brought in under the terms of the first Old Age Pensions Act passed in 1908. The dinner was held in January 1909 in Taylor's Victorian Café, organised by the Saffron Walden Men's and Women's Liberal Association, of which Taylor was a supporter. The photograph was taken by Horace Mansell.

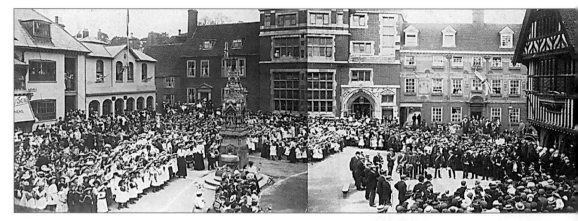

The celebration of Empire Day, 1908. All the schoolchildren in the town attended; the small children in a
line to the left of the fountain are from the Museum Street Infant School. Ernest Pitstow is conducting the
band.

As befits the centre of the town the Market Place has been the scene of a huge range of events. This is the
occasion of the declaration of the poll in June 1901, after a by-election had been called owing to the
sudden death of Armine Woodhouse. The Liberals won with a majority of 792 over the Conservatives;
Joseph Albert Pease became MP for the Saffron Walden constituency.

School journeys have been a feature of education throughout the twentieth century, both of schools in the town going elsewhere and non-local schools making the trip to see the town. Unfortunately there is no data with this picture to give any more detail on the origin of the group of both children and adults. The Greyhound pub, the Saffron Walden & District Co-operative Society shop and the entrance to the Co-operative Hall are clearly visible. The photograph was taken by Davies, *c.* 1925.

The War Savings Committee standing outside the Corn Exchange to publicise War Savings Week, March 1918. Left to right: Archibald Hamilton Forbes (borough surveyor), Guy Maynard (museum curator), Samuel Wenman (bank manager and amateur photographer), Hubert Collar (Liberal agent and future museum curator), Addy Nunn Myhill (mayor), Peter Giblin Cowell (farmer and borough councillor), David Miller (baker and borough councillor), C. H. Youngman (bank manager).

Bayonet instruction, 1918. This was held in Audley Park by 'B' Company, 7th Volunteer Battalion, the Essex Regiment.

Machine gun instruction, also by 'B' Company, 1918. Both photographs were taken by Underwood.

Walden Place was taken over as a Red Cross hospital for injured soldiers in 1915. The museum is fortunate to possess an album of photographs compiled by the nursing staff during the life of the hospital from 1915 until 1919. This is a picture of the second convoy of soldiers injured at the front, taken in June 1915.

Sergeant A. Selfe and Sergeant H. Cook, September 1915.

An open air tea party in the grounds of Walden
Place, July 1915.

The troops entertaining each other with a minstrel show, 1917.

The first Remembrance Day for the dead of
the First World War, held on the fourth
anniversary of the outbreak of war, on
4 August 1918. The fountain in the middle
of the Market Place is being used as a war
memorial. At this time, no end could be seen
to the conflict; consequently the Roll of
Honour has not been completed, a gap being
left even for the year when the war was to
end. The photograph was taken by
Underwood.

The commemoration of the first Armistice Day, 11 November 1919, in front of the Town Hall,
photographed by Underwood. Pride of place has been allocated to a captured German field gun. This was
later put on display on a concrete plinth outside the museum, later still requisitioned as raw material for
the Second World War. The Roll of Honour has now been completed with dates and names. Until
recently it hung in the parish church, but was replaced in November 1996.

The Town Hall sand-bagged during the Second World War.

The Presentation of the Freedom of the Borough to Brigadier-General Jesse Auton, Commander in Chief of 65th Fighter Wing of USAAF. The procession is in Market Street, on its way from the Town Hall to the parish church. Jesse Auton is accompanied by R.A. Butler, MP. Proceeding in front of the mace bearer is Councillor Stanley Wilson. Behind the two guests of honour is the Recorder, followed by the Mayor, Alderman Fred Goddard.

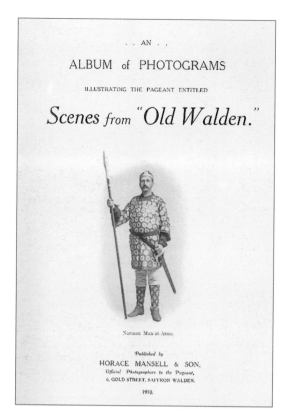

Title page of the souvenir booklet accompanying the Saffron Walden Pageant, May 1910. The idea for the pageant arose from meetings between staff of the Friends School and others, including Guy Maynard, the curator of the museum, who designed the costumes.

A plate from the souvenir booklet. This is one of the tableaux presented in Bridge End Gardens – British tribesmen making submission to the invading Roman army and presenting hostages.

The Saffron Fairies, also in Bridge End Gardens. Note the hollow globe on a pedestal in the left background. The pedestal is visible in the shot of the Gardens on page 85 minus the metalwork.

The morris dancers and a rather menacing looking herald, complete with hobby horse and inflated goat's bladder. Both of these photographs are taken from the souvenir booklet.

The Snowflake Laundry float before it had received its prize.

The carnival procession, 1920s. The Snowflake Laundry float received second prize. It looks a good deal more orderly than 1990s processions! Note the sign for the Greyhound.

The Pampisford Ales float put together for the special carnival that was held to celebrate the coronation of George VI in 1937.

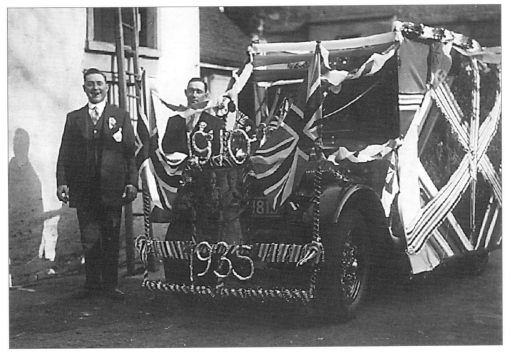

Goddard's float for the carnival procession in celebration of George V's silver jubilee, 1935.

The horse-drawn Women's Institute float getting ready on the Common for the silver jubilee procession in 1935.

The Saffron Walden Hospital float for the 1935 silver jubilee procession. A gruesome practitioner sits above an enigmatic legend which proclaims 'Out for the Kings Bounty'.

The waggon-way in King Street through to
Hart's printing works, 1913. It was then and is
still a good central fly-posting site, presumably
at that time for posters printed by the firm!
(See also the picture on page 38.) The cinema
had only been open for a year or so: see the
photograph on page 56. Other posters
advertise a lecture about the Stockwell
Orphanage by the Revd Thomas Spurgeon of
Thaxted Baptist Church.

The corner of High Street and George Street, c. 1910. I imagine the photographer had set his camera to take
a view of the Greyhound pub on the corner; the horse-drawn fire-engine about to round the corner from the
fire station in George Street was a bonus! The glass negative of this photograph is in the museum.

Cricket in progress on the Common, c. 1922. The Common was used for playing cricket from its earliest days in Walden in 1812 until after the Second World War, when the Anglo-American Playing Fields were created. The pavilion was moved there in 1954. The Saffron Walden Cricket Club was established in 1859, although the scoring details of matches that were played as early as 1823 between the town and Sawbridgeworth exist in the archives of the museum.

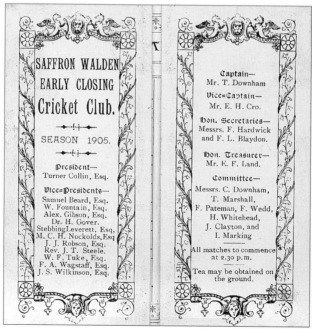

Cover of the match programme for 1905 of the Saffron Walden Early Closing Cricket Club. Like most small towns, there was no shortage of clubs and societies, which often led to rival clubs being founded. Although I have no evidence that there was any undue rivalry between clubs, it is noticeable that in the fixture list there is no mention of a match against the town's main club.

PEOPLE

In keeping with the somewhat self-effacing character of the town, no one single individual has stamped their personality on Saffron Walden. Instead, a number of highly idiosyncratic personalities have contributed; from the steely Saxon, Ansgar, keeper of the Tower of London, and the turncoat Geoffrey de Mandeville who ended up on the wrong side in the twelfth-century civil war, to Sir Thomas Smyth who wrested the town's hard-won rights back from the crown in 1549. The best known eccentric was Henry Winstanley, born in the town, who as well as devising spectacular water fountains in Piccadilly, created many practical jokes in his house in Littlebury for his hapless guests.

In the nineteenth century the beneficence of the Gibsons has been well-documented and well deserved. But what of the contributions of others? Gerald Penn, the clock man from the lower depths, peg-leg Auger, and other Walden families, like the Porters, Players, Pitstows, Coes, Dixes, Silletts, Robsons. All have made their mark, as the photographers on these pages testify.

A group of elderly inhabitants of the town on the lawn of Edmund Birch Gibson's house at 53 High Street, probably *c.* 1855. There is no indication of who they are, but they may be staff of the Gibson household. They are certainly dressed in 'Sunday best', some elements of which, the tall top hats of the men and close bonnets of the women, belong stylistically to the 1840s. This photograph was possibly taken by a Mr Porteous, who was a member of staff of the Saffron Walden and North Essex Bank, subsequently Gibson, Tuke and Gibson's Bank.

The Town Band, Bridge End Gardens, 1903. J.E. Galley of London Road took the photograph, and is also in it, in the middle of the back row. The Pitstows are much in evidence; the Bandmaster, centre of the seated row, being Fred senior, with the reversed sash, and the long faced clarinettist to his left, Fred junior.

The staff of the Friends School, 1917. The headmaster, John Edward Walker, is seated in the centre; C.B. Rowntree, deputy head and author of *Saffron Walden then and now*, is also seated. It would appear that smiling was not encouraged at this time.

Dr Henry Stear, medical practitioner in the
town in the late nineteenth century, local
councillor at various times between 1863 and
1910 and mayor in 1902–3. He was a noted
donor of pottery, especially Staffordshire
figures, to the museum. The photograph was
taken by W. Frost Wilson.

George Nathan Maynard was curator
of the museum from 1880 until 1904.
He completely reorganised the
displays in the 1880s, brought the
records of the collections up to date,
including superb drawings of the
objects; these are still in use today.
The family came from Whittlesford in
Cambridgeshire: his father was a keen
collector of geology, while his son,
Guy, grew up in the museum, took
over as curator in 1904 and later
finished a distinguished career at
Ipswich Museum.

John Thomas Frye who was organist of the
parish church for over sixty years, from 1824
(when he was twelve), until his retirement
in 1884. This photograph was taken by
W. Hobbs, possibly on Frye's retirement.

William Murray Tuke, partner in the Gibson,
Tuke and Gibson Bank, which joined with
others to form Barclays in 1896. He lived for
over thirty years in The Vineyard, indulging his
taste for fine pottery and porcelain. He
bequeathed many pieces to the museum, of
which he was a trustee.

The Mace-bearer John Evenett and the Sergeant at Arms George Moss Taylor, *c.* 1900. The two small maces were made in 1549 to commemorate the granting of the charter by Edward VI which created the first form of borough council. The great mace being held by the Sergeant at Arms is a very fine specimen, presented in 1685 as a 'reminder' to the council at the time to encourage them to adhere to the Catholic Church.

Portrait of John Brand, Saffron Walden's letter carrier and postman, *c.* 1890. He worked from the post office in Market Hill from about 1867, moving with it to King Street (see print on page 48) until he died in 1900. This photograph was taken by Walter Francis.

A travelling knife grinder at work outside the museum, *c.* 1964.

Saffron Walden Fire Brigade, photographed to show off their new uniforms, *c.* 1870. This photograph was taken by W. Sweeting of Holloway, London.

Hubert Collar, curator of the museum, when he was mayor, 1946. He is with Cliff Stacey, the town clerk, on the right. They are examining the mayor's badge outside the Town Hall.

The workers at the Dix & Green Cement Works in West Road, backing on to the railway station goods yard. They were photographed by W. Frost Wilson.

Ralph Dix, aged about eighteen months, in an early push-chair. He later worked in Sierra Leone, returning in about 1920 to become a teacher, and eventually headmaster of Hatfield Broad Oak School. His cane, with which he was closely connected with many of the village schoolboys, is in the Saffron Walden Museum collections.

Workmen associated with the Dix family cement business, c. 1912. The two seated men are Joseph Dix, founder of the firm, on the right, and Arthur, his son, on the left.

Joseph Clarke as a young man, drawn in 1850 by
D. Fabronius. Joseph Clarke was an antiquarian
and honorary curator of the museum for over
fifty years until his death in 1895.

The Roos Farmhouse, Debden Road, with Joseph Clarke standing outside, *c*. 1890. The Clarke family
owned large amounts of land in and around the town and were successful maltsters.

Three maids of the household of Miss Mary Gibson at Hill House, 1906 or 1907.

Portrait of Joshua Clarke, brother of Joseph and mayor in 1846, 1853, 1860, 1866–9, 1871–3, wearing the gold chain presented by him to the borough in 1873 and still worn today. The photograph was taken in 1873 by F.T. Day.

Celebration of the return of Private Ryan, Sergeant Pitstow and Private Lindsell from the Boer War, May 1901. The three men are seated behind the table. Alf Pitstow was one of Fred's sons. Fred is looking over the shoulder of the man standing behind his son. This photograph was taken in the Corn Exchange. Many of the respected inhabitants of the town were in attendance: Dr Atkinson, mayor, Dr Stear, William Adams, town clerk, R. Williams, job master, Mr Nockolds, solicitor.

Portrait of James Coe and his family of Debden Road, *c*. 1905. The image of the small boy on the left with a stick has been added. It is possible he had died not long before this photograph was taken. The two young men standing at the back were killed in the First World War.

Boys British School, *c*. 1908. Headmaster Harry Hayes is on the right.

ACKNOWLEDGEMENTS

The photographs on pages 51, lower, and 81, lower, are reproduced by kind permission of the *Cambridge Evening News*. The upper photograph on page 64 is reproduced by kind permission of Ian Stratford. All other images are the property of Saffron Walden Museum.

The introduction contains elements from my article in the Saffron Walden Directory, 1996. Thanks partner!

The direct or unwitting help of the following in the preparation of this volume is gratefully acknowledged: Stephen Bassett, John Cox, Maureen Evans, Martyn Everett, Jean Gumbrell, Cecil Hewett, Gillian Holman, Bruce Munro, Donna Sharp, Dave Stenning, Cherry Vanoli, Malcolm White, Mary Whiteman, as well as all past curators of Saffron Walden Museum. In common with anyone who seeks to write about the history of Walden, I owe a debt to the late Cliff Stacey, former town clerk and local historian with an unsurpassable knowledge of the town. I like to think he would have approved of this book, but know that were he living, he would still be giving me the detailed benefit of his many certainties.

Len Pole, 1997

BRITAIN IN OLD PHOTOGRAPHS

Lincoln
Lincoln Cathedral
The Lincolnshire Coast
Liverpool
Around Llandudno
Around Lochaber
Theatrical London
Around Louth
The Lower Fal Estuary
Lowestoft
Luton
Lympne Airfield
Lytham St Annes
Maidenhead
Around Maidenhead
Around Malvern
Manchester
Manchester Road & Rail
Mansfield
Marlborough: A Second Selection
Marylebone & Paddington
Around Matlock
Melton Mowbray
Around Melksham
The Mendips
Merton & Morden
Middlesbrough
Midsomer Norton & Radstock
Around Mildenhall
Milton Keynes
Minehead
Monmouth & the River Wye
The Nadder Valley
Newark
Around Newark
Newbury
Newport, Isle of Wight
The Norfolk Broads
Norfolk at War
North Fylde
North Lambeth
North Walsham & District
Northallerton
Northampton
Around Norwich
Nottingham 1944–74
The Changing Face of Nottingham
Victorian Nottingham
Nottingham Yesterday & Today
Nuneaton
Around Oakham
Ormskirk & District
Otley & District
Oxford: The University
Oxford Yesterday & Today
Oxfordshire Railways: A Second
  Selection
Oxfordshire at School
Around Padstow
Pattingham & Wombourne

Penwith
Penzance & Newlyn
Around Pershore
Around Plymouth
Poole
Portsmouth
Poulton-le-Fylde
Preston
Prestwich
Pudsey
Radcliffe
RAF Chivenor
RAF Cosford
RAF Hawkinge
RAF Manston
RAF Manston: A Second Selection
RAF St Mawgan
RAF Tangmere
Ramsgate & Thanet Life
Reading
Reading: A Second Selection
Redditch & the Needle District
Redditch: A Second Selection
Richmond, Surrey
Rickmansworth
Around Ripley
The River Soar
Romney Marsh
Romney Marsh: A Second
  Selection
Rossendale
Around Rotherham
Rugby
Around Rugeley
Ruislip
Around Ryde
St Albans
St Andrews
Salford
Salisbury
Salisbury: A Second Selection
Salisbury: A Third Selection
Around Salisbury
Sandhurst & Crowthorne
Sandown & Shanklin
Sandwich
Scarborough
Scunthorpe
Seaton, Lyme Regis & Axminster
Around Seaton & Sidmouth
Sedgley & District
The Severn Vale
Sherwood Forest
Shrewsbury
Shrewsbury: A Second Selection
Shropshire Railways
Skegness
Around Skegness
Skipton & the Dales
Around Slough

Smethwick
Somerton & Langport
Southampton
Southend-on-Sea
Southport
Southwark
Southwell
Southwold to Aldeburgh
Stafford
Around Stafford
Staffordshire Railways
Around Staveley
Stepney
Stevenage
The History of Stilton Cheese
Stoke-on-Trent
Stoke Newington
Stonehouse to Painswick
Around Stony Stratford
Around Stony Stratford: A Second
  Selection
Stowmarket
Streatham
Stroud & the Five Valleys
Stroud & the Five Valleys: A
  Second Selection
Stroud's Golden Valley
The Stroudwater and Thames &
  Severn Canals
The Stroudwater and Thames &
  Severn Canals: A Second
  Selection
Suffolk at Work
Suffolk at Work: A Second
  Selection
The Heart of Suffolk
Sunderland
Sutton
Swansea
Swindon: A Third Selection
Swindon: A Fifth Selection
Around Tamworth
Taunton
Around Taunton
Teesdale
Teesdale: A Second Selection
Tenbury Wells
Around Tettenhall & Codshall
Tewkesbury & the Vale of
  Gloucester
Thame to Watlington
Around Thatcham
Around Thirsk
Thornbury to Berkeley
Tipton
Around Tonbridge
Trowbridge
Around Truro
TT Races
Tunbridge Wells

Tunbridge Wells: A Second
  Selection
Twickenham
Uley, Dursley & Cam
The Upper Fal
The Upper Tywi Valley
Uxbridge, Hillingdon & Cowley
The Vale of Belvoir
The Vale of Conway
Ventnor
Wakefield
Wallingford
Walsall
Waltham Abbey
Wandsworth at War
Wantage, Faringdon & the Vale
  Villages
Around Warwick
Weardale
Weardale: A Second Selection
Wednesbury
Wells
Welshpool
West Bromwich
West Wight
Weston-super-Mare
Around Weston-super-Mare
Weymouth & Portland
Around Wheatley
Around Whetstone
Whitchurch to Market Drayton
Around Whitstable
Wigton & the Solway Plain
Willesden
Around Wilton
Wimbledon
Around Windsor
Wingham, Addisham &
  Littlebourne
Wisbech
Witham & District
Witney
Around Witney
The Witney District
Wokingham
Around Woodbridge
Around Woodstock
Woolwich
Woolwich Royal Arsenal
Around Wootton Bassett,
  Cricklade & Purton
Worcester
Worcester in a Day
Around Worcester
Worcestershire at Work
Around Worthing
Wotton-under-Edge to Chipping
  Sodbury
Wymondham & Attleborough
The Yorkshire Wolds

To order any of these titles please telephone our distributor, Littlehampton Book Services on 01903 721596
For a catalogue of these and our other titles please ring Regina Schinner on 01453 731114